Lean Enterprise Institute

Instituto Lean Management

Other titles in the **Follow the Learner** series:

The Lean Dentist: Establishing one-piece flow in patient treatment, by Sami Bari, DDS

Follow the Learner

The Lean Bakery

Eliminating waste to get closer to your customer

by **Juan Antonio Tena** and **Emi Castro**

with **Roberto Priolo**

Lean Enterprise Institute, Inc. **Instituto Lean Management**
Cambridge, MA USA **Barcelona, Spain**

September 2017

Lean Enterprise Institute

© Copyright 2017 Lean Enterprise Institute, Inc. All rights reserved. Lean Enterprise Institute and the leaper image are registered trademarks of Lean Enterprise Institute, Inc.

ISBN 978-1-934109-53-3
Design by Thomas Skehan

Lean Enterprise Institute, Inc.
215 First Street, Cambridge, MA 02142 U.S.A.
Tel: 617-871-2900 • lean.org

Table of Contents

Foreword by Oriol Cuatrecasas

Introduction

1. The Problem to Be Solved

2. Improving the Work

3. Bringing Lean to the Shops

4. The Ultimate Shop Experiment

5. A Different Managerial Culture

6. How We Experiment

Conclusion

About the Authors

About the Institutes

Foreword

Around a year ago, Juan Antonio Tena called me to discuss his latest experiment: making all the bread a 365 cafe needs—and perhaps even the pastries—in the workshop of each shop. I couldn't believe my ears, and asked him if he had really thought this through. After all, in the 365 bakery factory it only took three people and one machine to produce the 12,000 to 19,000 loaves of bread the business sells each day. Surely, making bread in each 365 shop would cost more!

In response to my skepticism, Juan Antonio playfully said: "If the quantity of flour, water and bread starter is the same, and if the energy we use to produce one baguette is the same, then the only thing we need to think about is making the processes more efficient, no? Here we go, a bit of work to keep ourselves entertained! Besides, shouldn't you be the one advocating for smaller batches and getting closer to the customer?"

Oh my, what a lesson I was taught that day. He was completely right, of course. We didn't know how to get there, but we had a challenge on our hands. Another one.

Indeed, Juan Antonio always has invaluable lean lessons, and over the past few years, he has become one of my teachers. (I have had a few, starting with my father Lluís—the author of *Volver a Empezar*, the book that first brought lean to 365.)

I also remember vividly how, when lean process improvement was first brought to the shops, Juan Antonio's wife and business partner Emi Castro kept repeating that she didn't want her *niñas* (the saleswomen) to lose their joy of selling. She always proved eager to get her hands dirty and show them, time and time again, how to work with colleagues and how to serve customers. She never lost her temper and determination, not even when facing the strongest resistance (this is easier said than done). Although I must admit she did tell me off once or twice for using "bad words" (Japanese terms) with her girls.

"Enough with the Japanese. Things are over complicated only when we make them so," she would tell me. She is a specialist when it comes to understanding how lean can initially take people aback and how one can help them to understand. She has taught me a lot in this sense. I recommend you follow her advice very carefully.

I am not a character in the story told in this book—just a very fortunate spectator, and at times, an advisor for all the crazy, yet fundamental lean experiments 365 has and continues to run. But as a spectator, I have the privilege of knowing all the characters of this lean tale, and I would like to introduce them to you.

We have Arantxa, the engineer who with intelligence and perseverance, first helped lean take root at 365. (Did anyone tell you it takes years?!) And then we have Eva and Conchi, the two extraordinary shop supervisors who took it upon themselves to translate the experiments we devised into meaningful PDCA for the shops and the people working in them. (Deming would have been proud!) And then Agus, the restless and never-satisfied Operations Manager who finds any gaps that open up and that we struggle to close. Finally, Unai, the engineer who, as production manager, painstakingly tends to the "365 machine" to ensure it never stops working and improving.

Studying an organization like 365 isn't easy, and describing it in a book isn't either. The first time I read this manuscript, I had the impression that the transformation had been described in a way that some could deem simplistic. I really feared that readers in more complex—or different—situations might be prejudiced against this story.

However, looking back at my experience with 365, I quickly realized that the only "simple" thing about their story is the way in which the team was able to see their processes and current state—through the previous veil of complexity—and to create a strong vision of what 365 could become. Lean teaches us to shed the unnecessary and simplify, to extract the essential, and then work tirelessly to improve it. As you'll find out in this book, that really isn't easy.

I hope you'll let the "365 spirit" inspire you—you won't regret it. Enjoy the book and, who knows, maybe even some of the 365 products during your next visit to Barcelona!

Happy reading and *bon profit*.*

Oriol Cuatrecasas
Insituto Lean Management
Barcelona, Catalonia, Spain

---

*_Enjoy your meal_ in Catalan.

Introduction

We have a saying here in Spain: "*A pan duro, diente agudo.*" Literally, it means, "When the bread is hard, use your sharpest teeth." Loosely translated, this proverb encourages us to tackle difficulties with the right tools.

Running a business is no walk in the park. The worries, the responsibility, the daily problems, the long hours—no matter what type of business you are in, whether health care or manufacturing, retail, or software development, you are likely to face difficulties in your day-to-day life.

The business I am in, as the proverb might suggest, is bread making. I am the owner and CEO of *365.café*, a family-owned chain of bakery shops in Barcelona. We began this business in 2000 and have built it into a thriving enterprise employing around 400 people. Each day in our 100* shops we sell thousands of loaves of bread, pastries, cakes, and sandwiches, to mention but a few of our products. We produce most of our daily supply of bread and pastries in a bakery factory—our *obrador*—located west of the city center. Having opened more than two dozen new shops in the past two years, we find ourselves currently experiencing an unprecedented rate of growth.

It wasn't always like this, of course. We have certainly had our fair bit of business challenges to overcome. To paraphrase the proverb, when my wife Emi and I started the business, we thought our teeth were sharp enough, but we were wrong.

*at the time of publishing

During the first few years, we were working extremely hard, but it wasn't enough. What we needed was a system to control our processes and make informed decisions on the next steps. That system turned out to be lean thinking, which has been at the core of our work for the past decade and has brought us great results. It has completely reshaped our culture, changed our business, and fueled our growth. Every day it opens new doors for us—showing us the way to go and making us a little bit better.

Many excellent examples of lean thinking can be found throughout the business landscape, so when Instituto Lean Management and the Lean Enterprise Institute asked me to write this book, I didn't quite know what to think. At 365, we spend so much time looking at the problems we find that we often forget about the good things. Sometimes it takes someone from the outside to tell us how far we've come since we opened our first bakery factory in a former barn. I had to take a step back and look at the bigger picture to understand why our story is worth telling.

What makes us so interesting is perhaps the fact that we are applying lean to something as run-of-the-mill and yet atavistic as the *making of bread*, the most elementary of foods. Or maybe it is the fact that we have cleverly managed to turn our bakery into a hyper-efficient factory supplying dozens of shops every day. Or maybe it's the incredible growth we have experienced, which has almost doubled the number of shops we have in the past five years.

Yes, the more I thought about it, the more I realized the many achievements we could use to present our story to the lean community. But what I think is really worth learning from our experience is our utmost belief in the power of experimentation; the things we have tried and the many mistakes we have made over the years have led us to where we are today.

We always hear that lean is a journey. I believe that at its core, it is a journey of experimentation, of continuous discovery, and of new and better ways of doing things. Our approach to lean is very practical. We don't use many Japanese words, and we don't always apply the methodology by the book. We have learned to live and breathe the fundamentals, and we work hard to adapt the tools to our changing needs and circumstances.

When I say "fundamentals," I mean turning waste into value, which can be achieved only by focusing on customers and respecting employees. This is the basis of our approach to management, which we complement with the knowledge that we gain each time we solve a problem or make an improvement.

My sincere hope is that you will find this book inspirational and useful in further advancing your own lean journey.

Juan Antonio Tena
Barcelona, Spain
2017

1. The Problem to Be Solved

One night in 2012, we received an unexpected visit. All of a sudden, the police surrounded our factory and asked us to show them the "secret entrance to the basement." They were convinced that we were employing illegal immigrants, and despite my telling them it was not the case, they insisted that they come in. They moved all the machines and spent hours looking for a basement that doesn't exist, before apologizing for their mistake and leaving.

Weeks later we found out they had acted on a tip-off. Our competitors couldn't believe that a factory as small as ours could produce so much and of such high quality. They thought we had illegal immigrants hidden underground working 20-hour days. Instead, what we had was an amazing system to organize our work—in plain view. That system is called lean thinking.

In a way, I can see how they would think we were cheating. The transformation we have undergone is massive, and sometimes even I find it hard to believe that a 7,000-square-foot factory can bake enough artisanal bread and pastries to supply 83 shops. What we have been able to achieve is extraordinary, especially considering how different things were when we started off and how full of obstacles our journey has been.

And yet, as impressive as our turnaround might seem, people who visit us often say that lean is "real" here: to new challenges we respond with new changes, and we never stop improving and evolving. Our approach to change is based on running experiments and learning from them, and when you view our journey from that perspective, you will see why lean thinking was the right option for us.

But before we delve into what we did to transform the organization, I think it's important to briefly take you through the history of 365 and explain the problems we had been experiencing before we discovered and ultimately applied lean thinking to our processes and way of working.

How 365 Came to Be

I have been in the business of serving people for most of my life. When I was 12 years old, my family opened a café in Barcelona, called Bar España. I often helped my parents at the café, working with my mother in the kitchen and sometimes waiting tables. I enjoyed the contact with customers, but what I really loved was the work that went on behind the scenes in the kitchen—the true heart of the café.

The process of preparing food fascinated me, and I liked the idea that people could come in, eat what we made for them, and leave happy. My parents' work ethic was solid, and customer needs always came before everything else. For example, in the first few months we often received a call in the middle of the night from road workers who were paving the nearby streets, asking if we could prepare something for them. And we did. We went downstairs, opened the café, and started cooking—often for dozens of people at a time—at 3 in the morning.

The family business: son Agus, Juan Antonio, daughter Leonor, and Emi

Perhaps my parents' desire to do well was a consequence of how hard things had been for them in the past. My family left the Extremadura region to seek fortune in Catalonia when I was only a year and a half old. Life in much of Spain had become extremely hard after the Civil War of 1936–1939, but the city of Barcelona and the surrounding area had remained relatively prosperous, thanks to its industrial infrastructure and access to the sea.

The presence of large industrial groups boosted the growth of the city. SEAT was one of Barcelona's largest employers at the time. It was considered something of a Holy Grail: people saw a job at the carmaker as steady income and a secure position for life. My parents wanted that for me—every parent in Catalonia wanted that for their child—and sure enough, upon returning from mandatory military service, I found a job at the company.

I worked at SEAT for a total of six years, as an apprentice at first and then as a production line worker making small metal components. I didn't mind the job, but I am a pretty restless person—a trait inherited from my father—and the comfortable 9-to-5 job soon began to feel like a constraint.

What I really wanted to do was go back to working in the family business and at some point even start my own company. So when SEAT eventually realized it had hired too many people and started to offer its employees the opportunity to leave and a severance package, I took the money and ran, so to speak.

At that time, my family was running the Bar España, in addition to a coach operator and a number of repair shops for coaches. (We are quite the entrepreneurial family.) I spent six years doing all kinds of jobs in the family businesses, until we decided to add another tile to the mosaic and opened a bakery. We didn't produce our own bread, we bought it from other bakeries and resold it. Business at the bakery seemed to thrive.

However, we had too many projects going and we relied too heavily on bank loans. When the economic crisis of 1992 hit we couldn't borrow more money to invest in the business and trouble ensued. The next five years were extremely difficult, as the business started to slowly but inexorably sink.

We were then running seven shops across Barcelona. In 1995 I had a fallout with my family and took over the ailing bakery business. But despite having fought hard—mostly by myself—the family shops drew their last breath in 1997.

Going through bankruptcy and being left with nothing were traumatic experiences. I struggled to come to terms with the fact that the business had failed, even though it had appeared to do well for so long. What had we done wrong? How had it happened? These questions kept nagging me and a sense of apprehension—not to mention guilt—started to grow in me.

I didn't see it at the time, but I now realize that we may have had the determination and a strong desire to succeed—we sure worked hard, day and night—but we lacked the necessary understanding of how to run a business. We knew nothing about accounting, purchasing, sales, etc., and had no process or methodology to guide us. In other words, we didn't have a solid basis on which to build our company.

Luckily, I am a very determined person—some would say stubborn—and more importantly, I am not afraid of trying new things and making mistakes. So I dusted myself off and decided to start all over again. In the meantime, I had met my wife Emi, and in early 2000 we opened a new bakery together.

I may have tried to fight it, but bread making is what I love and where my experience is, so it made sense to go down that path again. That's how 365 was born. Little did we know that 15 years later we'd be running a citywide chain of 70 shops, 55 of which are franchises, with great prospects of growth.

An Epiphany

As far as humble origins go, I think 365 takes the cake. When Emi and I started off from zero in 2000, we operated out of a former barn. At the front was a small square room, connected to the production area in the back by a narrow and very long corridor. At the time, we weren't even selling bread on site—that came later when I realized it was silly not to sell, when we had a space overlooking the street—but simply delivered it using a friend's tiny old car.

We had so little money at the beginning that we didn't even have a compressor fitted on most of our freezers. At times, we struggled to pay for our weekly 500-kilogram supply of flour. Today we use around 4,500 kilograms of flour *every day*. To think of the growth we have experienced over the years still makes my head spin sometimes.

Space in the barn-bakery was so limited that each night we had to disassemble the shop at the front and use that space as a warehouse. We used to load the shipping trucks right in front of the building, using two little counters on wheels placed one next to the other as a loading dock. All in the same place we would bake the bread, let it cool off near the door, package it, and load it for distribution. Only in the final three years in the old barn-bakery could we afford to rent an adjacent space overlooking the back street. Moving the loading activities there made things easier for us, as the van didn't have to stay parked in front of the entrance to the shop.

We had nothing at the beginning, except the determination to make it. We were driven by our desire to succeed, our passion for running a business, and, quite frankly, by our need to put food on the table—there is no incentive quite like it.

We worked night and day with dedication and enthusiasm, but the memory of the hardship I had previously endured was still fresh in my mind. As 365 took its first steps, I felt the same sense of apprehension I'd felt after the family bakeries had gone bankrupt. I began wondering again how something seemingly successful could go down the drain so easily, especially after you put your heart and soul in it. I grew increasingly restless and convinced myself that the answer was out there somewhere, which encouraged me to look for a solution. I didn't want to go through what I had in the wake of the 1992 crisis.

By 2003, we had three shops and I had the idea to start making coffee in one of them. People were a bit reluctant. ("A bakery is a bakery; a café is a café," they would say). But the experiment turned out to be extremely successful and we replicated that model in the other two shops.

It was becoming clear, however, that the more the business grew, the more complicated things got. We were working all day long, seven days a week. The only family time we had was a late lunch on Sunday in the only place with a kitchen that was still open at 4pm, a Chinese restaurant.

But this wasn't the first time I had done so much hard work, and I was painfully aware that it would not be enough to keep the business afloat, let alone make it a success. I realized that we couldn't keep opening shops without having a proper system in place that could give us the foundation to support the growth of 365. I didn't want to leave things to chance, so I started to read every book on business and management that I could find, including every book by Eli Goldratt.

In 2003 I read *Lean Management: Volver a Empezar* by Lluís Cuatrecasas, then president of the Instituto Lean Management. This book tells the story of a company's journey from traditional management to lean management. It provided a framework that I could potentially follow to try to bring some order to the way we worked—and hopefully put my anxiety to rest.

I knew that the ideas suggested in *Volver a Empezar* wouldn't solve all our problems. But I knew there had to be something more than just hard work, sweat, and tears to make a company successful. That book was telling me that "something more" was lean thinking. The novel showed me the way, but it was still a novel, and it didn't tell me how to practically apply lean. I wasn't confident enough that I could do it, but my curiosity was now alive and actively pushing me to learn more.

Meanwhile, 365 was growing fast, and my sense of unease was growing with it. In 2004 we had six shops and a year later the number had risen to nine. At that time, we started to plan for what I often called our *obra faraónica*—our "pharaonic project"—to expand the production area of our factory. This entailed expanding to the upper floor of the building, installing a freight elevator, and buying a number of freezers. This type of investment was massive for a small company like ours.

A Momentous Purchase

As it happened, right before starting the expansion work, we went on a five-day vacation to Galicia—we hadn't been away in years. At the airport bookstore, instead of grabbing a thriller that would have surely gotten my mind off work, I decided to buy a chunky hardback book titled *Lean Thinking*. I'm sure you can relate to this, the fact that I would be away didn't mean that I couldn't still think about work.

That book was one of the most important purchases I have ever made. I read it cover to cover in a heartbeat; it was like a light went on in my head. What I loved about it was the fact that it was full of examples of real companies achieving real change. *Lean Thinking* seemed to complement what I had learned from *Volver a Empezar*. At this point, I realized that lean thinking was the foundation 365 needed, and reassuringly, I now had a way of applying those ideas.

During the vacation, I couldn't help but think that the big investment to expand the production area was a bit reckless and perhaps not necessary just yet. I realized we could improve so much in the factory first. The moment we got back to Barcelona, I called off the project and started to take my first steps toward a new, leaner system.

Lean brought us the most extraordinary and radical changes I have ever witnessed in a business. The incredible rate of growth we have experienced would not have been possible without lean. In 2005, when we started to apply lean thinking, we had nine shops around Barcelona; today we have 100.

We are not perfect, and the gears often screech, but lean has no doubt given us a completely different perspective. Every time we are unsure, we have something to turn to. The methodology doesn't give us answers, but it provides us with the tools we need to get to those answers ourselves.

Over the years, I learned that if a company is to thrive it needs a strong system in which people can blossom—besides hard work, spirit of sacrifice, and an iron will. Indeed, this is the answer to one of my existential questions.

Sadly, my restlessness is still not completely cured. I have actually never stopped looking for more. Sure, lean has made 365 more flexible, agile, and adaptable. But even now that we are implementing it across the whole organization—from the factory to the shops—I still keep my eyes wide open. There is no guarantee that what works today will still work tomorrow. Isn't there always a better way of doing things?

2. Improving the Work

In this chapter, I would like to explain what happened when we started to run the first lean experiments at 365 and how quickly and dramatically things changed. I will then take you on a tour of our current factory and describe our processes in detail. This will help you to understand what lean thinking has allowed us to accomplish and how we were able to grow so much and so quickly. You might think that a lot of what we have done is simple and nothing more than common sense. We often feel like this ourselves … in hindsight.

A Better Way of Doing Things

When I first discovered lean, capacity was one of our main problems: our freezers were too small and we simply had too much to put in them. They filled up very quickly, and storing all of our products had become a nightmare. You know your factory has problems when remaking a particular product becomes easier than retrieving it from a freezer because it's buried under a million croissants and cakes. We found it even harder to admit that we had no way of knowing exactly how fresh a loaf of bread was.

With the exception of baguettes, which we made every day due to very high demand, we used to produce and freeze a week's worth of products every day. On Mondays we would make enough croissants to last seven days and freeze them, on

Tuesdays we'd produce *cañitas*, on Wednesday, *xuixos*, and so on. As if that weren't enough, our process also entailed baking the products at the factory prior to shipping them.

Our system had seemed perfectly logical to us for a long time, even though batching actually created endless problems in production and required a lot of storage space. Whenever a freezer got full, we'd store part of a batch in another one—only to forget it was there.

As much as we seemed to be convinced that the quantity of products we had to prepare wouldn't change the amount of work we had to do, the more shops we opened, the harder it became to keep things running. It's like how cooking dinner for you and your spouse takes barely half an hour, but preparing dinner for a big group takes the whole afternoon, even when you are making the same dish.

The big batches were making it impossible for us to control our processes. The lack of visibility over the work made matters even worse, because nobody knew what we had produced or where we had stored it. One of our bakers could all too easily blame the late completion of a production run on a missing ingredient, even when that wasn't the case. Additionally, the shops were running short of products all the time, even though what they needed had probably been produced, but it was either work-in-progress or hidden somewhere in our inventory.

Our answer to these problems was, of course, to produce more. We were under the impression that big batches would allow us to gain control over our processes, when in fact they simply caused bigger problems. For instance, if you forget to add salt to bread for a small batch of 50 loaves, it is one thing, but if your batch is 500, it is quite different.

It became impossible to understand the current state of the work in the factory. Were we producing enough? Were we producing on time? What sequence of tasks were we following on the shop floor? What problems were we experiencing? Whenever I tried to ask our pastry baker Albert one of these questions, his answer was always the same: "Sorry, Juan Antonio, I really can't talk now. I have a lot of work to do."

Bakers and machines in the first factory, running at full steam!

Indeed, we always finished work late, as the to-do list for the production team grew longer and longer and our inventory ballooned. We paid huge amounts of overtime and had a brutal capacity crisis building in the factory. The situation was very frustrating and made me really uncomfortable.

Why did we always seem so busy? How was it possible that we never had a moment to stop and reflect? Why were we all so stressed out, always in the middle of a crisis, and unable to communicate with one another to find ways to improve?

In *Lean Thinking*, I found a possible way out of this troublesome situation. I became determined to start experimenting with the advice provided by the book, to try and make our operations more efficient and finally solve our problem with space. If anything, I saw this experiment as something worth trying before we conceded to the apparent logic of expanding to the upper floor of the building.

One of the first things lean taught me was that batch-and-queue is a bad idea and that one should strive to create flow instead. Womack and Jones defined it as "the progressive achievement of tasks along the value stream so that a product proceeds from design to launch, order to delivery, and raw materials into the hands of the customers with no stoppages, scrap or backflows." It made sense that my first experiment would be to change our approach to production to help our pastries flow more easily through the process, from when they are nothing but flour to when they are placed on the counters of our shops.

The First Few Experiments

I still remember the day I tried to run my first lean experiment. I walked into the factory and said: "I want to try something new. Today I want us to produce all the types of pastries we need for tomorrow; only those we need tomorrow."

Silence fell in the production area. If we had been in a cartoon that would be a tumbleweed moment. People looked at me as if I had gone completely crazy. They thought that making thousands of several different products every day, rather than thousands of the same product for a whole week, would add unnecessary complexity to our already-chaotic processes.

Before the first experiment: a factory corridor full of products.

I didn't know it at the time, but this was a turning point in the history of 365. Despite the reluctance of some workers, we tried the experiment of running small batches for about a month. Before long, our freezers began to empty, and our capacity problem gradually disappeared. Suddenly things seemed simpler and crystal-clear.

I then realized that I could go one step further and try a second experiment, to find out exactly how many people I needed to complete production for one day. Perhaps I could find a way to reduce or eliminate overtime.

I went to the workers and said, "Please make whatever we need for tomorrow and then go home. I will pay your full day's wage, of course, but I want you to go as soon as you are done."

Again, their faces betrayed utter disbelief. Clearly hesitant and with many questions in their minds, they went back to work. After about two hours they all left. The machines stopped, the hustle and bustle ceased, and the factory went eerily quiet. The following day we repeated this experiment. Once again, we sent people home as soon as they completed production for the next day. And we just kept going like that for a couple of weeks.

The first few days were very difficult as we adapted to the new system. Workers would hide in the factory because they didn't want to leave the factory! Yet I didn't want to use them to produce what we didn't need. They were astonished that the boss didn't want them to use their time to the fullest. They were ready to do overtime if necessary, but not this.

As exciting as the experiment was, I was of course torn. On the one hand, this was something I really wanted to try—as you probably understand by now, I like to see my decisions through—but on the other hand, people were telling me I had lost my mind.

At one point even my wife Emi, who had always been one of my staunchest supporters, asked me, "What are we doing, sending workers home after one hour?"

She worried that we were asking too much of our employees, especially considering that they had stood by us through all the challenges 365 had faced the first few years. Apparently, some of them went to her and asked whether they should be looking for another job, while others even encouraged her to talk to me because I had "gone crazy."

I was aware that this experiment could very well make things more complicated for us, but I also knew that we had to understand the work if we were to be able to improve it. How many workers did we need each day for production? What tasks were they supposed to carry out and when? How long did it take them to complete them? These were some of the questions I aimed to answer when I decided to run the second experiment.

Over the course of a few days, I started to notice that it was taking only two hours to produce all the croissants we needed for the following day. Previously, the process normally stretched over a whole day. At that moment, I realized that a lot of waste was hiding in our processes, the small batches were just making it easier for us to see it. Work could be completed in less time, and the production process could be streamlined to facilitate waste removal.

August proved to be a good time to run this experiment, in the summer things are not as busy and our production volumes are lower. However, as soon as schools reopened in September, things went back to their normal rhythm and we had to make many more products. But now we had a new approach and a more stable processes, with flow being introduced and people working regular eight-hour days—which made overtime a thing of the past.

These first steps toward lean thinking taught us the importance of simplifying processes to unleash the power of flow. We discovered that batching was interrupting the flow and creating a lot of waste in the form of overproduction and excessive movement. Why did we need to move the product to a million different places in the factory? Why did we have to complete all those actions when only a few of them actually added value to the product? We started to ask many whys and eliminated all the waste we could find, to the point where we hardly needed any freezers.

Seeing Results

With no external help and no practical lean knowledge of my own, all I could do was focus on one experiment at a time, in a trial-and-error kind of way. First came the production schedule, then sending the workers home. Soon, and much to my delight, our problems began to disappear, one after the other. Every issue we managed to fix encouraged me to keep going, no matter how disgruntled some of the workers had seemed at first. I was truly learning by doing and gradually chipping away at my fears and reservations—and at our stock.

It might seem silly, but our space problem had kept me up at night for so long that I almost couldn't believe that lean had made it so easy and quick to fix. Right there and then, after the first few experiments, that accomplishment is all I could think about. Not only was this dramatic change solving our overtime and space-related problems, but also it helped us to break our processes in smaller, more manageable parts.

Suddenly, we became aware of the work to be done each day. We learned that Mondays are slow, weekends more difficult, and so on. Critically, instead of having a seven-day process to somehow figure out, we now had seven standardized one-day processes to complete. Bottlenecks disappeared and we regained control of our production. I had to push a bit at first to get the bakers to follow the lean path, but in the end they understood that this was the best way. The system we put in place still acts as a huge poka-yoke for production: so long as we follow it, making mistakes is extremely difficult.

As we tackled one problem at a time, we were able to create enough efficiencies in our processes to constantly postpone the beginning of the expansion project. "Let's start in two weeks," I would say—only to push plans back another fortnight or even a month later. After about a year, I realized that I had postponed the expansion for so long that we didn't even need it anymore. Instead of investing, we could just continue to improve!

I now had months of experience solving problems at the gemba on a daily basis, and evidence that the improvements worked. It wasn't long before I understood what is perhaps the biggest lesson lean thinking has ever taught me: rather than big changes, ==it is preferable to concentrate on small, incremental improvements==.

Because there is always a better way of using one's resources, one doesn't necessarily need to jump to the (perceived) big and quick solution. Before I read *Lean Thinking*, we were ready to invest a ton of money to expand and purchase new machinery.

Once we started to live into the idea that improvement is incremental, all the pieces started to fall into place. When I halted the Pharaonic project it was 2005. Four years later, we had *three times* the number of shops and *half* of our freezers were empty on a regular basis. We managed to stay in that same "small factory" until we opened shop #33 in 2009.

Timeline for 365

Year	Total shops	Own shops	Franchises	Important events
2000	1	1		First shop opens
2001	2	2		
2002	3	2	1	First franchise opens
2003	6	4	2	Juan Antonio reads *Valver a Empezar*
2004	6	4	2	
2005	9	4	5	Juan Antonio reads *Lean Thinking*
2006	17	6	11	
2007	25	6	19	
2008	30	6	24	Arantxa starts coaching
2009	35	7	28	Move to new factory
2010	37	8	29	Lean thinking introduced to the shops
2011	39	8	31	
2012	45	8	37	Production manager with lean experience hired
2013	51	11	40	Upgrade shop concept
2014	53	12	41	
2015	69	15	54	New lean shop model

A Factory That Runs Like Clockwork

In 2009, we finally moved into a new factory. The two years before the move were spent planning and working out the blueprint. I had a man helping me, he had worked all his life in the world of bakeries, making bread machines and arranging for the installment and creation of bakers' workshops across Spain. I asked him to design the new factory, even though we hadn't found a place yet. He didn't seem to love the idea, but he decided to humor me anyway. He was just a couple of years away from retirement, and he must have thought, "Why not?"

We met every Saturday to work on the project and, from the very beginning, he seemed to struggle with the way I was approaching the creation of the blueprint. Normally, you have a space of a certain size and form, and given the constraints, it presents potential locations for rooms and machinery.

But I was going about it the opposite way. I wasn't interested in seeing where pillars or walls would be. I thought only about the work and how we could ensure it would flow with no interruption through the facility—no matter what it looked like.

After some time working together, the bakery designer and I had gotten pretty close. One day, while looking at the blueprint, the man cleared his throat and said: "Juan Antonio, there is something I need to tell you that I really feel bad about. For months and months, I thought you were completely insane."

There you go, another person calling me crazy. A bit taken aback, I asked him why.

"I set up bakeries all over Spain all my life," he explained, "and I never thought that a few months before retirement I'd meet someone who wanted to design a factory that didn't even exist yet. I must say, though, I now realize that you were right all along. I understand what you were doing."

We eventually found the right space with a rather strange shape: a triangle! Surely, our factory is likely to be one of the most peculiar gembas you will ever see—and not just because of its shape. (*See factory map on page 32.*)

In a bid to optimize space and better utilize our resources, we have learned to move things around all the time. We have been in our current factory since 2009, and I can't tell you how many times we have changed the layout. Imagine what it is like for our South American workers, who often go away to visit family for a month and a half at a time! They come back and have no idea where things are.

At first, lean people walking into our triangular factory might think they have gone to the wrong place. The first impression is not exactly one of a working space that has been thoroughly "5S-ed" or where lean is applied in earnest. But you shouldn't judge our book by its cover. As soon as they see us in action, they realize that 365 is actually lean to its core. It depends on a system that runs like clockwork: every single inch of space has its purpose, every room a prerogative, every person a role.

Factory Tour

I would like to take you on a tour of the factory, to show you what we do and where. I will share examples of improvements we have made and describe how we use our very limited space. Hopefully, this will give you a sense of what our processes are like and make clear why we cannot afford any slip ups.

First, let's start by looking at the floor plan of the factory. The triangular shape is pretty unorthodox! (*See page 32.*) We are located in the middle of the Pedrosa industrial area, west of Barcelona's city center. The shop floor is on the first level, our offices are upstairs. The total floor area of the building is just under 7,000 square feet.

It might sound like a lot, but it's not when you consider that we supply most of our 83 shops from this single facility. Every day we produce around 15,000 baguettes (9,000 prebaked and 6,000 frozen), 2,000 ciabattas, 12,000 croissants, and up to 1,000 cakes. In total, we deliver a staggering 270,000 products daily.

Upon walking in, you immediately see a wall completely covered with shelves that hold all the nonfood products the shops need, e.g., napkins, plates, cleaning products, boxes for cakes, plastic bags, etc. The factory is the only supplier for the shops, everything comes from here.

Straight in front of you, you find a stack of white plastic boxes; these are the clean ones that we use to deliver the bread. There are dozens of them, positioned just outside the tunnel through which they are cleaned.

We have a very sophisticated visual system in place to distinguish clean boxes from dirty ones: when they are flipped, they are clean, when they aren't they're still dirty. Each box carrying bread has a tag attached to it. This tag shows basic information on the delivery, such as the shop the box is to be sent to, how much of each type of bread, and so on.

Next to the box tunnel is the machine we use to make our mixes for different types of breads and cakes, which we recently moved from the warehouse to save space. Peek inside and you will see the bread mix being prepared: it's made of flour, salt, yeast, and bread starter (known in Spanish as *masa madre*), all carefully premeasured to obtain the desired outcome.

You are now in the heart of the factory, where you can find our *tren de laboreo*, the "train machine" we use to make baguettes. It is extremely versatile. You can change its settings, such as weight, speed, and shape, depending on the type of bread you want. It consists of four machines, each connected to the next like a train:

- kneading machine (*amasadora*)—You pour the mix in and add water and some extra flour. The ingredients are then mixed through hundreds of revolutions per minute. After 12–15 minutes, the dough is ready for the next step.
- weighing machine (*pesadora*)—The batch of dough is divided in pieces, which are then weighed with precision.

- proofer (*cámara de reposo*)—After all the high-speed mixing and molding they endured, the balls of dough relax and soften for 20–25 minutes. This part of the process—when the yeast first becomes active—is when we really add value to the bread.
- forming machine—After a few minutes, the piece of dough is rolled, to squeeze out the bubbles of air, and given the right length and shape.

Once the baguettes come out of the forming machine, each tray, carrying 10 of them, is placed on a cart, which is then transferred to the fermentation room—our factory's proofer.

In the case of ciabatta bread, the baker and not the machine (*chapatera*), adds most of the value. It's a different process altogether: the dough rests not in a machine but in boxes stacked one on top of the other, for an hour and a half. After that, the baker places the dough in the chapatera, which cross-laminates it and gives it the right height.

The ciabatta workstation used to be located next to the train machine and worked between 8–10 hours each day. However, when we had to find some extra space to install a freezing machine, we had an idea: to combine the ciabatta production area with the croissant production area, given that the two processes never took place simultaneously.

When the overnight production of ciabatta is completed, we take the chapatera away and bring in the machines and folding tables we use to make the croissants by hand during the day.

Bakers making croissants by hand on folding tables.

It's like moving assembly lines in a flexible single space. If a line is not used, is moved away. This has saved us enough square meters—we can use as many as we can get—to install a new freezing machine, while ensuring that the area is now in use between 16–20 hours each day. A much better use of space! (Even though not everybody loves moving machines around, they create simpler machines, which pushes efficiency).

The new machine, which uses nitrogen to freeze some of our bread—we call it ultra-bread—was a very important investment. Even though we pay more than we would for mechanical freezing, this machine is extremely practical, as it can freeze 900 baguettes in 30 minutes while preserving their quality, in a way that common mechanical freezing cannot do.

Factory map and process steps for baguettes

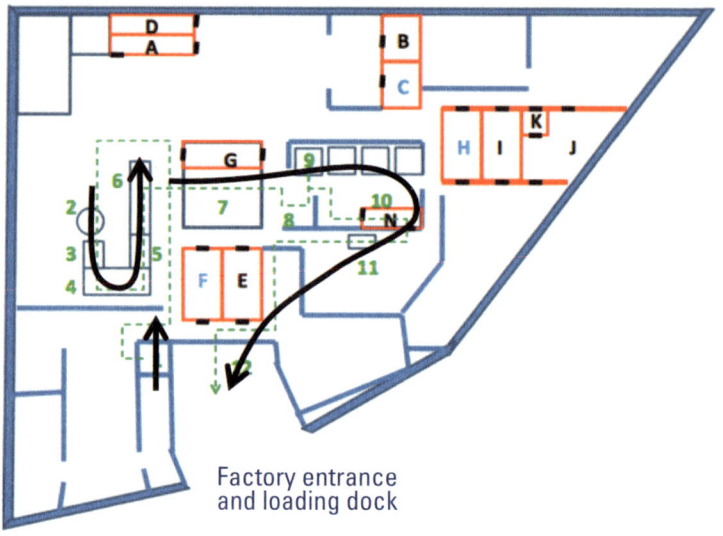

Factory entrance and loading dock

1. Pre-mixing
2. Mixer
3. Divider
4. Rest + Former
5. Traver
6. Proofer
7. Cutting
8. Oven
9. Cooling
10. Packaging
11. Transportation

Process steps of croissants

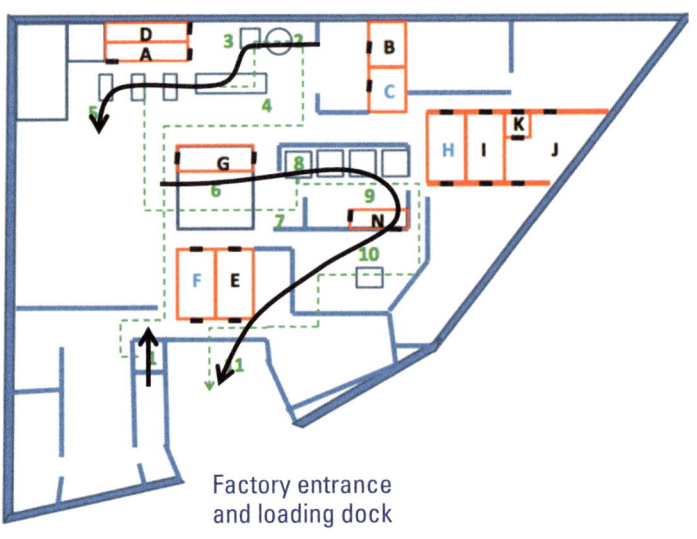

Factory entrance and loading dock

1. Pre-mixing
2. Mixer
3. Divider
4. Lamination
5. Former
6. Proofer
7. Decoration
8. Oven
9. Packaging
10. Picking
11. Transportation

Historically, we were delivering the bread prebaked to the shops. But we have realized that the highest possible quality can only come from proofing and baking the bread in the shops. It's during the proofing that the quality of the bread increases. Unfortunately, we have limited space in the factory and our proofer is not big enough to accommodate 9–12 hours of fermentation. We are slowly moving the proofing process to the shops, by providing them with frozen, rather than prebaked, bread. Each shop has two proofers, in which the bread ferments overnight; this process increases its quality exponentially.

Let's continue our tour of the factory. If you turn right at the croissant/ciabatta production area, you will find yourself in the section where we make pastries (*bollería*) in the afternoon and cakes (*pastelería*) in the morning. Making pastries requires a lot of handwork.

For example, to fill a *caña* with chocolate, chefs normally use a pastry bag. Because every pastry contains the same quantity of filling, we tried to speed up the process by using a pastry-filling gun. But before long, we realized that the improvement was not that lean, because it took a long time to clean the gun every time we needed a different type of chocolate. So we simplified the device as much as possible, removing unnecessary parts and replacing the inner tube that carries the filling. Most of our changes are fairly simple but incredibly effective.

Adjacent to the bollería and pastelería areas are the ovens. We have only a handful of them and thousands of products to bake every day. This forced us to come up with an efficient way to use them: we manage a flow of trolleys in the corridor leading to the ovens by lining up four of them at a time, always in the same sequence. The first three trolleys carry bread, the fourth one carries pastries.

With this system, trolleys enter and leave the ovens one-by-one. All that people have to do is drag them into the room and push them out once the products are baked, this creates a clear pull system for each section. Depending on the product, the oven time ranges between two and half and three and a half hours. There is no confusion.

Trolleys in queue and about to be removed from the ovens.

Just outside the ovens, we have an extraction fan to accelerate the cooling of the products. When they come out of the oven they are piping hot, much too hot for picking. The temperature of the room is enough to bring the products down from 200 to 50 degrees (Celsius), but to lower the temperature to the desired 25–30 degrees more quickly, we need to park the cart under the fan for about 45 minutes.

Many of the rooms in the factory have different uses at different hours of the day; that's how we manage to produce so much out of such a small factory. I shared the example of how we use the same space for the production of ciabatta bread and croissants at different times of the day. There is another important instance in which the use of a room changes during the day: the picking area, which is adjacent to the ovens.

Like everything else in our factory, the warehouse/picking area is small and serves multiple purposes. It's where we receive goods from our suppliers in the morning and load the products to be delivered to the shops at night. In the afternoon, this space is used as a temporary warehouse for croissants, and at night for order picking for the shops.

At first, our suppliers had trouble understanding our system. They insisted on delivering full pallets, instead of half pallets or just boxes because, "it is cheaper." But we didn't have enough space for all those goods at once. Even if we had, moving and storing them would have cost a lot of money and resources. We didn't want the hassle of having to manage that process and, more importantly, we didn't need that many goods at once.

Another large problem we faced was the bottleneck that occurred on Fridays when we would receive supplies for the whole weekend. 365 works seven days a week, but most of our suppliers only deliver Monday to Friday. We don't have enough space to hold products in the warehouse for three days. So at first, we began to use pallets to store goods—mainly those we don't make in the factory like soft drinks—on elevated shelves in the room where we load the trucks. The pallets were organized by day, and all we had to do on Saturdays and Sundays was bringing them down and load them onto the truck.

Items in the warehouse area.

Segmenting supply like this helped us to balance the intake of products and eliminate bottlenecks. In addition, we've asked our suppliers to show up at 12pm, rather than 6am, so that order picking could begin as soon as we received the goods, which therefore spent as little time here as possible. We have now gone one step further: when we receive goods, we directly fill the boxes that will go to the shops without storing anything. This process is completed by three people instead of one.

Recently, we have introduced a new system for the picking operations: we call it the *shopping cart*. The person responsible for filling the trolley with all the products to be shipped uses a small computer and a pair of earphones to go through the list of items. One-by-one and in the right sequence, based on where products are stored on the shelves, a computer voice tells people what they need to pick next. Once they have grabbed the correct item and say "OK, "the computer advances to the next item. This prevents us from skipping products to be shipped, which causes shortages for the shops, irritates the customer, and forces us to arrange emergency deliveries.

Over the years, we have run countless experiments with shipping. At first, all the shops received supplies and products at night, but as the network grew this became increasingly challenging. We then decided to ship twice a day instead: in the afternoon we'd supply the shops with the durable products, like cans of soft drinks, while at night we'd supply the perishable products, which, of course, had to be as fresh as possible for customers in the morning.

This meant doing more rounds and spending more time on delivery, but at least we were able to supply all the shops without experiencing too many problems. Because storage on site is a big problem due to space constraints, over time we have learned to dispatch products two or three hours after they are produced—which lowers the number of urgent deliveries we have to complete (anything a shop might need can simply be sent out with the next delivery).

Picking items in the shopping cart

These days, as the process in the shops gets more stable, we are trying to move back to one delivery per day, starting in the afternoon and finishing around 4–5am. We try to get the quantities right every day so that we don't need to supply anything extra. However, we maintain a buffer of two or three hours each morning for emergencies, when one of our drivers travels around Barcelona to deliver whatever extra items a shop might need—even something as small as a can of soda or a pack of sugar.

Critically, delivering in small batches every day means our shops don't need a lot of storage space. Instead, they can accommodate more tables (rather than piles of products). This lowers our overhead costs (less rent for smaller shops and less inventory-related costs) and increases revenue, which we then use to invest and grow.

Returning to our tour, at the end of the warehouse you'll find our kitchen. Here we prepare food to be sold in our shops, as well as to people working nearby (we deliver lunch to their offices). Kitchen shelves are replenished every day using a kanban system, which has a very visual and mistake-proof way of seeing what's missing from our pantry: a wire traveling overhead across the room.

When a new order comes in, we write it on a piece of paper and clip it to the wire. The order will then move across the room, from station to station, as the process unfolds: cooking, warming up, packaging.

At the last station—the last stage in the process of preparing a dish—the piece of paper is pulled from the wire and stuck to the package. That same sheet will be used for shipping. This is one-piece flow at its finest.

A Small Factory to Stay Lean

What makes our factory so different is the unique use of space, which varies at different times of the day. Over the years, we have mastered the art of adjusting to an evolving situation and learned to optimize the use of space and resources—creating continuous "pull" for further improvements.

We have become very crafty and creative, developing an ability to modify tasks and moving machines and activities around—sometimes it feels like a life-size game of Tetris. We adopted this approach in our first factory to encourage a more efficient use of space and what we had on hand.

Originally, we thought we'd have to move out by the time we opened shop #11 due to capability constraints. Thanks to our lean system, we scrapped the pharaonic expansion project and managed to stay put until we opened shop #33. If you need further proof of how impactful our lean improvements have been: the freezer space we had in the barn-bakery was larger than all the freezers we currently have—combined.

Back in 2009, when we moved to the new factory, we thought we would be able to use it to supply 60 to 70 shops. With the introduction of standards, continuous improvement of processes, and the optimization of space, we now believe that we can comfortably supply up to 110 shops.

This facility has changed more than we ever thought it could, yet we know we can do many more things to improve it and make it more efficient. It essentially reached full capacity around two years ago, but we are still opening new shops. How is it possible? Simple, we are not opening them in batches!

Because we open one shop at a time, our production manager, Unai Abrisqueta knows that approximately every three weeks he has to "make space" for one extra shop, whether that means carving some time out of the croissant-making process or changing the delivery time of soda cans. He knows to come up with new ideas for small improvements.

One could be tempted to simply move to a larger production facility, but I don't plan on doing so until it becomes absolutely necessary. We managed to stay in the barn-bakery for years after we began implementing lean and we can do the same now. I am aware of the opportunities for improvement and growth that we still have here and know that we can easily supply another 25–30 stores out of the current space before we need to start worrying.

But more than anything, I am not keen on the idea of moving to a larger space; because I know that a larger space means more opportunities to create waste. When we moved to our current facility, we forgot about lean for a while and started to make mistakes again.

We had gone from having no space at all to having a lot, relative to the number of shops we had to supply. I couldn't believe that we were having more problems in the new factory than we had in the old one, in the face of higher capacity and similar volumes. We had fallen into the trap of comfort.

More space made us lose focus on improving and streamlining processes. When space was limited, we keenly felt the need to find a better way of working and to make the most of what we had. Having very little space forces you to be creative and to never let your guard down.

For example, we currently carry around 1.5 days' worth of production in our facility, which means that if there is a glitch in the system, we risk not being able to supply all the shops. The mechanism has to always work seamlessly. This is a very strong incentive!

Perhaps the biggest lesson we have learned from this experience is that comfort is lean's worst enemy. Having space, extra people, access to a lot of money, etc.—all of this is at odds with what lean stands for. The methodology is made for situations where the money is little, the space is tight, and demand runs high. You need a crisis to make lean stick.

Being 365's Production Manager

Prior to joining 365, I worked for a multinational organization that eventually closed its Spanish operations and moved production to China. It looked like lean was applied in earnest there, when in reality it was just checklists and standards imposed on people. Everything looked great on paper, but deep down people were not convinced. And how could they be, when management itself wasn't convinced?

At 365 things are much different, because management really believes in lean and knows how to communicate it. There is no better way to explain lean than in a practical ways. Juan Antonio often uses examples from everyday life to get people to understand the message. It's only in practical applications that people see that lean works; otherwise, they tend to interpret it as some abstract philosophy, or worse, a temporary fad. The reason why 365 is a success is that people here want to implement lean because they understand that it can—and will—help them.

When I started here, before I began to implement changes, I had to get to know my people and learn how to deal with them. Naturally, I have kept my office downstairs, on the shop floor, because that's where I need to be.

Every day, the first thing I do is go on a gemba walk, sometimes just to say "Good morning, how are you?" or "Do you need anything?" and sometimes to help workers with actual problems they are facing. These first 15 minutes of the day are the most important for me.

A critical part of my job is to listen to people and observe them, to talk with them about their problems and learn from the solutions they come up with. This is the only way to gain their trust and to ensure they join you on the lean journey. People must feel comfortable talking about their problems, whether they're job-related or happened at home. This is the single most effective way to create a team aligned on a shared goal. Transforming groups into teams is perhaps the most important outcome—and at the same time, the biggest enabler—of a lean transformation.

Perhaps the fact that we are a small company works to our advantage. At 365, people work closely with one another, know processes really well, and perhaps find it a little easier to work in teams than they would if they were in a larger organization. The fact that we don't have bureaucracy and that silos are not as strongly defined here as they are in your average corporation creates an ideal environment for team-based problem solving and for cross-functional collaboration.

There is another great benefit of being a small company with few extra resources and little money to spend: we are never tempted to pick the most expensive solution assuming it will be the best one; instead, we always work to find the smartest one.

Unai Abrisqueta
Production Manager

3. Bringing Lean Thinking to the Shops

by Emi Castro

I have always loved to sell. It's what my family did before moving to Catalonia; we were fishmongers in Granada. Clearly, it has brushed off on me. Unlike Juan Antonio, the interaction with people is what I enjoy most. However, I am an old-school seller, so the things I have learned from lean over the years had to be shown to me a few times before I could fully understand them.

At one point, when the factory had already put lean in place and the shops hadn't, it was like we were running two separate businesses. The factory was Juan Antonio's battleground and the results he was achieving there spoke for themselves, but in the shops I wanted things to go my way.

To me, every shop was different. One needed this, one needed that; one had a particularly difficult clientele, another needed an extra person for things to run smoothly. How could we possibly impose one way of working on so many unique environments? At one point, though, the shops started to cost too much money: some of them had five or six employees, and the expenses of the retail side of the business were ballooning. And so seven years ago, around the time we moved to the new factory, we realized that we had to bring lean thinking to the shops as well, and that created a bit of conflict. It's always like that when you try to change things, isn't it?

I really struggled at first. Whenever Arantxa Moya, our first lean coach, came to one of the stores to see me, I always found an excuse for not being there. Lean thinking scared me, and I was very doubtful. In particular, I was worried that the experiments would get in the way of customer service.

In the factory, customers don't see what we are doing, but in a shop, they do. I didn't think it was a good idea to stand next to the line to measure the time a customer had to wait to be served. But the truth is that we needed experiments like that, and when we finally ran them we discovered things we never could have imagined. For example, it turned out that people waited less in shops with two employees and a solid working system than they did in shops with three workers but poorly organized processes.

Before lean improvements were implemented in our shops, people's roles were not very well defined. The employees said they were part of a team, but in a team everybody has a specific role to fill and knows what that role is. Helping each other doesn't mean that we all need to do everything.

For example, I had the bad habit of always going behind the counter to work and serve customers myself. I thought I was helping, until Arantxa one day told me I couldn't do it anymore. I was not happy about it, and I certainly didn't want anyone telling me that I couldn't sell in my own shop.

But then she said something that, while obvious, I had never thought about before: "There will come a time when you won't be able to be physically present in all the shops. There will come a time when you won't be able to sell in all the shops. And then what?" That's when I understood that I had to take a step back and start observing.

Arantxa had every reason to try to limit my attempts to micromanage, because she had been doing a fair bit of observing. One day, she stopped by with her little daughter. We sat down at a table with two of our supervisors, Conchi Escuder Moya and Eva Fernandez Llagostera. I asked Eva to go in the back and get a croissant for Arantxa's daughter. She went but didn't come back. I then asked Conchi to go, and she too disappeared.

At that point, Arantxa and I looked at each other and I said, "Where have they gone? What's up with croissants here today?"

I went to the back of the shop myself to see what was going on and before I knew it, I had joined Eva and Conchi, who were helping to prepare sandwiches for the day. The three of us were slicing salami and helping at the cashier, completely oblivious of everything else.

At that point, without us knowing, Arantxa joined the rest of the customers in the very long line stretching along the counter. When Eva called the next customer in line and saw Arantxa in front of her, she stopped for a moment and said, "We are not doing well, are we?" That same day, Arantxa filmed them at work in the shop, later proving to them that they thought they were helping but actually weren't.

Separating tasks and creating boundaries had become necessary, and lean process improvements helped us do just that. I know how hard it was for everyone to understand and embrace lean thinking at first, but we're glad we did, because it is now clear how much it has really helped us. Without it, we would not have achieved all that we have. (And there is no doubt I could not have done it alone: Conchi and Eva's help, their passion and commitment to improve and their ability to connect with people have been absolutely instrumental.)

Before introducing lean, we didn't have any time to stop and think, because we always had something to fix or a crisis to avert. You can have a smile on your face and care for your customers, but if at the end of the month you have no money to pay your workers and suppliers, it all feels a little pointless.

Now we know what makes a shop work and we don't sweep problems under the rug. Now we have a system. So for example, when an employee asks for help and says that her shop needs an extra person, we have the tools needed to analyze the situation and determine whether an extra employee makes sense. And most of the time, we find there is no need for any extra people.

How the Shops Work

In our factory, either you engage with every person involved in the process or things stop working very quickly. We became aware of this in 2009 and realized that the only way for 365 to succeed would be to make the shops lean, too. We are now actively applying lean methods in all the shops we manage directly (15 of 70). When we decided to get started (the first lean shop was no. 35), Conchi and I were absolutely convinced that we could implement lean across all the shops within a week. We kept saying we could do it together, every day for a week: one shop in the morning and one in the afternoon.

Seeing lean improvements working so well in the factory had given us the *wrong* impression that applying it in the shops would be easy. I guess that Juan Antonio couldn't find it in his heart to rain on my parade.

Truth be told, introducing lean was fairly straightforward. Maintaining it and changing the culture, however, proved to be different matters. When you have been doing things a certain way for years it is very difficult to change. It takes time—definitely more than one week.

We set off on our journey to apply lean in the shops the only way we knew would make sense: by observing the current state. This was difficult to initiate because our approach as managers was very hands-on. It took a while for me to realize that my helping the employees by putting on an apron and getting behind the counter was actually a barrier to our improvement as an organization.

Things started to change once I understood how important it was for me to take a step back and open my eyes. We carefully observed how the employees moved around the shops, how long customers had to wait in line, and what the current process looked like (through value-stream mapping). We spent a lot of time learning to see problems and bottlenecks and the opportunities to improve them.

One day, Eva was carefully observing and taking notes on the current state of one of our shops. A customer approached her and asked, "Do you work here?" Eva nodded, to which the he replied, "I was getting really angry when I saw you sitting there and doing nothing, while your colleagues were struggling with such a long time. But then I realized you are observing the situation and writing down what you see—I am guessing you are doing this to improve things. That's great!"

While not a tool in itself, observation has been by far the most valuable lean practice we've learned. When we began to observe the work and track employee motion—on what we call

Shelves stocked for the morning rush.

spaghetti charts—we finally understood that the shops were very chaotic, roles were not defined, and everyone kept bumping into each other. Because employees didn't know their role, they were running around making coffee, working at the back, running the cashier, making sandwiches, and so on. They were doing everything and nothing at the same time.

The spaghetti charts showed how many steps they were walking every day—a lot! Let's just say that a long cardio session is nothing compared to the amount of effort our employees put into their daily work because of our poorly designed processes.

Spaghetti chart of cafe work

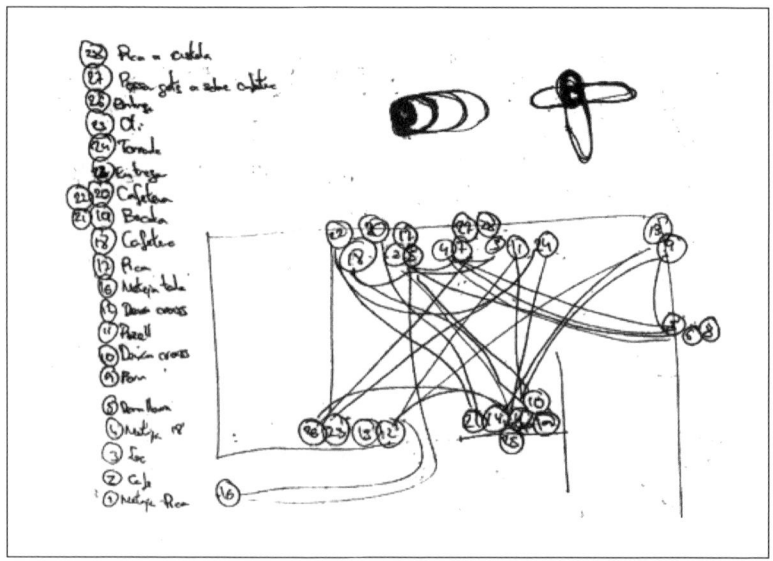

Not surprisingly, by the end of the day our shop workers were exhausted and very stressed out. To fully understand the impact on the well-being of our people, we brought the spaghetti chart to life by attaching wool thread to our workers. The ensuing tangle made it clear that they were running around all day long, victims of a process they hadn't designed and that was making their daily working life very difficult.

We decided to divide each shop into a number of areas and looked at the differences in the work in each of them. We defined what quality work looked like in the different areas—the cashier, the coffee machine, the display window, the oven in the back, etc.—and tried to understand how that related to how happy and satisfied our employees were with their jobs. Before we implemented this change, workers never had time to take a break—not even for lunch or a coffee. In a well run organization there should be time for everything, for work as well as for resting.

After we identified work areas and got an idea of how the work could be improved in each, we moved on and applied 5S. We had to clean up the place, which meant not only grabbing a broom and sweeping the floors—which of course was already happening—but also reorganizing the work space to make it easy for employees to find what they were looking for and to remove all the obstacles—both physical and not—preventing them from doing their job as efficiently as possible.

The implementation of 5S made us aware of a very painful truth: we had absolutely no idea how much we were selling or how long it took us to use up our supplies. For example, we used to have packs of water bottles stacked all over the place. "What are you doing with this much water?" Arantxa asked. The truth is, we had no idea.

We had to learn to really see, which would mean involving our employees—those who know the shops and the work best—to find better ways of doing things. We had to search for

Before lean improvement: water and products stored all over the shop.

the data on how many products we had in stock and why we thought we needed that many. It took us months to obtain all the information.

5S resulted in a new approach to organizing the shelves, what later becomes our pull supermarket. Every product, both on the shelves and in the refrigerator, now has a defined space, a code, and the quantity in stock is clearly visible. We never have fewer than one or more than three items available in the supermarket for most products. Replenishment happens when one piece is left, e.g., when a shop gets down to one bag of sugar or one pack of tortillas. Even then, the warehouse at the factory will only send two more, so that the maximum is always three.

Controlling orders and quantities has become much simpler. Pull orders are recorded on our IT system, which automatically communicates to the warehouse what items a shop needs. The system is so simple that if I see a shop has more than three items, for whatever reason, I know something has gone wrong. This helps us keep our stock low while increasing the visibility over what is used and how quickly.

As we write this, we are delivering products twice a day to all the shops that receive their bread from the factory. Delivery happens the day after the order is received, but we can also meet urgent needs should they arise. Of course, sometimes two deliveries are simply too impractical. We are going to open a shop in Figueres, some 150 kilometers from Barcelona, and that's going to receive only one delivery per day.

But let's go back to the organization of work in the shops. During the spaghetti chart exercise we divided each shop into working areas, which helped us to better define the specific roles and tasks for each employee in each area. We created three different types of workers, A, B, and C (most shops only have A and B), and defined standards for each of them. Standard work for each type is as follows:

- **Worker A** looks after "quick" tasks: staffs the cashier, works between the cashier and the display window, (which has to always be tidy and full of products with price tags clearly visible), sells bread, pastries, sandwiches, and beverages, and offers customers the opportunity to purchase additional products.

- **Worker B** works between the cashier and the coffee machine, covering the "slower" tasks: making coffee, collecting and washing dishes, and preparing sandwiches. She also takes care of everything in the back of the shop, from warehousing to using the ovens.

- **Worker C** works in the back, cleans the shop, and occasionally helps fill the display window. She performs the extra tasks that are not part of the typical A and B cycles.

In shops with only two workers, **A** works the counter and till, while **B** makes coffee and takes care of the tables and the back of the shop. If not too busy, **A** can help **B** perform certain defined tasks, like collecting and washing dishes.

Diagrams of A + B + C work areas and tasks

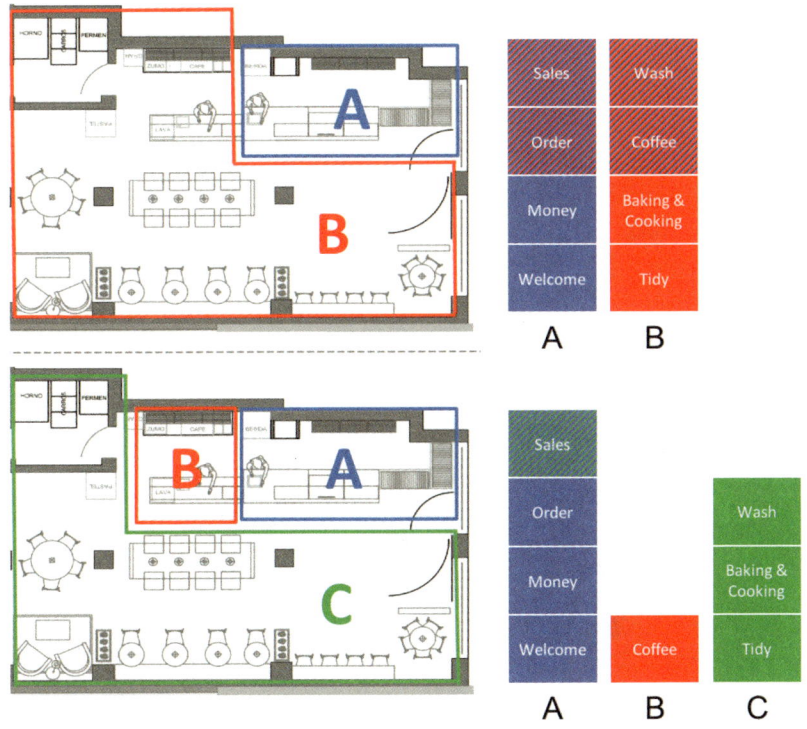

To teach the **A + B system**, at one point we had to place an actual table between the two areas to keep the employees separated. They just kept "slipping" and working on stuff their colleague should have been doing, trying to help, but really creating confusion.

3. Bringing Lean to the Shops

Once established, this A + B approach gave us better control over the work and allowed us to concentrate on how many employees each shop should have. We are no longer tied to the assumption that a shop needs three or four people to function properly. Each shop needs the right number of people, and through improving the system, we have learned that most of the time, that number is two.

We have stopped guesstimating and losing money on overstaffed shops. The number of employees we allocate to a shop depends entirely on its sales takt time. Even in a central area of the city, with lots of offices and many people coming for

Workers Poala and Romona in their A + B roles.

lunch, it is not uncommon for us to have only one-and-a-half to two workers per shift: one from 5am–1pm and one from 8am–4pm for one shift; and one from 2pm–10pm and one from 5pm–10pm for the second shift. Of course, this can vary greatly, depending on the shop and the day of the week. Everything is based on the takt time.

All employees at 365 can perform their tasks without having to ask for help or additional information. When in doubt, all they need to do is look at the standard work sheets and job instructions, which clearly describe what their job is and every important thing they need to know to make sure the shop runs as expected.

There is a standard for everything, including the quantity of food that goes into each type of sandwich. For example, a tuna sandwich will have a given amount of tuna, which is provided to the workers pre-weighed and ready to pick using tongs; the same with *fuet*, a typical Catalonian cold-cut. We had to weigh it all and calculate the measurements, but now we know that if we have sold a certain number of *fuet bocadillos*, we have used a certain number of packs of fuet. The numbers must always add up. When a shop has only one pack of an item remaining, they request replenishment. The factory will send two more packs, and those three packs should typically last for three days. Of course, some shops request products every day because they sell more.

These standards also they tell us how much of a product we need to produce and dispatch. We calculate this every week and keep an eye on the data of daily consumption. An additional benefit of this ordering system is that when a problem—or potential problem—occurs we know about it right away. For example, if a shop is using too much of a given product, we can understand why and act on the issue immediately. Having less products helps us to better control our shops.

Because the system is so clear, we know exactly what we are going to sell. We even reached the point where we were so precise in our forecasts that at the end of day the display windows were completely empty. It was a rather sad sight, especially for a shop, and we had to start supplying stores with a little more, just to fill the window a bit. (Whatever is left over at the end of the day is sent to a children's hospital.)

Proximity to the Customer

Just like it makes sense to make the employees' work easier and encourage them to come up with the solutions to their problems, it is also extremely beneficial for us to be as close to our customers as possible. In fact, I would say that the greatest amount of innovation at 365 takes place at the shops, because that's where we learn what our customers want. What they define as value guides our transformation and continuously points us in the right direction.

We involve our clients in our improvements and processes. Of course, during product development we invite them to product tastings and always consider their feedback and demands. This ensures that the products we manufacture are exactly what they want. There are also suggestion boxes in every 365 shop, asking our customers questions like, "What products would you like us to sell in this store?"

We always focus carefully on how our products are received in the market. Whenever we bring out a new pastry or type of bread, before unveiling it in all the shops, we try to sell it in one shop and analyze how it performs—in a way creating Minimum Viable Products (MVPs) to test, check, and learn.

When it comes to determining how much of each product we need to produce for our shops, our production manager makes the call. We use a forecast based on the past three weeks of sales: a formula calculates the amount we need to produce of each product in order to meet demand and avoid having an excessive number of returns, because everything that is not sold comes back to the factory. Other variables must also be taken into account, such as seasonal variation. July, August, and the first half of September are the worst months in terms of sales, because kids are not in school and families go on holiday.

The highly important variable of location can determine the success or failure of a shop—no question about it. When it comes to deciding where to open a new shop, we use a map of Barcelona to get a general overview of the situation and then move on to study the area in detail. Is the shop located on a corner? Does it overlook a big crossroads, with lots of people walking by? Is the street pedestrianized or mostly empty? Is it a residential neighborhood or in Barcelona's city center?

For us it's also extremely important to keep up with what the competition does. How much are they selling their bread for? How is their quality? As a result, if you come to our house, you'll find bread from pretty much every bakery in Barcelona—except ours!

From a financial standpoint, lean—coupled with Juan Antonio's ability to negotiate with suppliers—helps us keep our prices low and our quality high. It's like selling Prada pieces at Zara prices. Even though we have a very good quality/price ratio, however, we are not the only ones in Barcelona who serve good coffee and make good bread.

I believe that what differentiates us is the way we interact with our customers. I am absolutely sure our manners set us apart. We want our shops to become regular hangouts for people in the neighborhood, we want them to be places where people are greeted by an employee who knows their name and engages with them on a personal level. The shops—especially those that opened more recently—look young and hip, but this alone is not enough to make 365 the neighborhood café meeting point. For that, we need our employees to wow, charm, and delight our customers.

It's certainly happening, and 365 bags are becoming an increasingly common sight in Barcelona. The first time I saw one, I was at the beach and it felt incredible. I was so proud that I took a picture and posted it on Facebook.

The Experience of Two Coaches

Our mission as coaches is to walk with our people, motivating and guiding them through every step of the lean journey we are on together. For this to happen, we must ensure they understand what we are trying to achieve with lean and why we want them to be a part of it. We need to show them that we believe in them and in their capabilities, and that we are always there for them.

For this reason, we try to visit each shop once a week or once every 10 days, maximum. The system we use to assess shop performance allows us to quickly see what shop and team needs our help.

We have a number of ways to get an understanding of what is going on in our shops. The most useful is probably the "reviews" (or *auditorías*). Every shop fills out a checklist in the morning and another one in the afternoon. These help us to see the state of the work and understand a shop's internal dynamics.

Every time we visit a shop, we fill out our own checklist, which contains the same check items as the employees' list, plus 10–15 extra questions. We then compare this with the employees' review. Whatever differences we find are problems we will discuss with employees and at the weekly meeting with Emi, Juan Antonio, the shop managers, and the other coaches.

At the weekly meeting, we measure each shop's performance by looking at sales targets, number of customers, and average amount of receipts. We have a very simple and visual system in place to do it: depending on the results they have achieved in the previous week, each shop is positioned on the board in either the green area or the red area. This leaves no room for doubt. Green is good; red is not, no room for alibis. It's our way to quickly unearth things that aren't working and target them at management level.

However, it is the employees' help that we really can't do without—they are the ones working in the shops everyday. Every morning each shop manager holds a short staff meeting to discuss problems, analyze the current situation and targets, and of course, address worries or doubts people might have. This is when staff participates most actively, bringing up problems and making suggestions for improvement.

Thanks to lean, we have a system that allows us to detect problems more easily and quickly, and our people know they are allowed—in fact, encouraged—to flag them. If they didn't, how could we possibly improve?

Simpler, smaller issues are normally solved quickly by the team, often with the help of the shop manager. But whenever there is something they can't solve on their own, they can pick up the phone and ask for help. We are there to help them get rid of any obstacle they might encounter.

We want to know everything that goes on in our shops, no matter how unimportant it might seem. We have learned to track every problem and analyze every complaint, so that we can react quickly. If the person who delivers products to the shops inadvertently bumps into a window with a cart, we want to know about it. If a customer had their purse stolen, we want to know.

Having a clear idea of what goes on in the shops makes the work predictable: we know what's likely to happen and what to look out for. This way, there are no emergencies, and the staff never needs to panic.

Proactively reviewing what the day looks like and what problems might occur is the best way to approach the work. Do we have all the supplies we need? Were there any problems yesterday? Did the oven bake the product well? Is the shop full or empty? What's our sales target for today?

In our minds, there are two sides to each person's skills set: a technical one and an emotional one—what some might call "soft skills," like the interaction with customers or the ability to work in teams. Standards are there to make the technical side of the work easier, but it is our job as coaches to develop a person's emotional skills. This entails recognizing what our people do well, but also being honest in telling them what they can improve. There is no other way to develop them and help them to grow.

Some new workers when they start working with us, they feel lost. Here everything is different. They realise that most of their previous experiences have to be unlearned, and that makes feel them insecure on the job when they first begin. This is why we started what we call the "babies program". Every new employee has a manager that acts as their "mother," taking care of them, talking with them everyday, explaining and showing tasks—ensuring the "new babies" grow up healthy in their capabilities.

Teaching our people the importance of teamwork and respect for others is just as important to us as developing their practical skills. By doing all this, we hope that one day every 365 employee will be fully autonomous and able to solve problems without our help. We are working hard on making ourselves less indispensable.

Conchi Escuder Moya
Eva Fernandez Llagostera
365 lean coaches

4. The Ultimate Shop Experiment

As we write this, we have three types of shops:

- Those we supply with pre-baked bread—it is partially baked in the factory, delivered to the shop in plastic bags, and baked on site for another 12 minutes.
- Those that receive the bread dough frozen and ferment and bake it on site.
- Those that make the bread from scratch—this is a new model of shop which we are currently trying out.

We launched the new model shop in 2015, as an experiment. We have a baker make the bread on site and let people in the street watch the process. The back of the shop is visible from the outside—just like the open kitchen in a restaurant. The idea behind this experiment is to produce bread of a higher quality in requested mix quantities. In this new shop, the bread ferments naturally for 24 hours, which means we don't have to use much yeast and additives.

This is completely different from what most organizations in the food industry have been doing. For quite some time now, the prevailing business model has been to centralize operations in order to maximize economies of scale. But while you might spend less money to make large volumes of bread at a time, the complexity and cost associated with packaging, transportation, and logistics tend to make mass production not worth it.

Fast-food restaurants are another model. They may have revolutionized the industry with their simple and efficient assembly processes—burgers are delivered to you, you heat them up for three minutes and serve them to customers—but to do that they have had to sacrifice the healthiness of their products, using lots of preservatives, and so on.

This is all changing at the industry level: customer expectations and the culture around food are changing, people are starting to be more interested in locally sourced, organic, and healthier products. They want to know what goes into the food they eat, and who could blame them?

In the new 365 shops, there will be no secrets, no more bread made in the back of the shop or in the factory where nobody can see it but us—just healthy products made two meters away from the point of sale. Our idea is to go back to the old-fashioned way of making bread, one that will remind customers of when they were in their mother's kitchen. It's a familiar, homey feel we're after. We believe this will have a very positive effect on our image, as more and more people will be able to see and experience how our bread is made.

However, I would say that the most important element of this new experiment—possibly the biggest change our organization has ever gone through—is that we are bringing value creation as close to the customer as possible. This decision stemmed from the changing demands of our customers, but also from the direct and very clear correlation between waste elimination and moving closer to the customer.

Please allow me to elaborate. We all agree that eliminating waste means improving your organization and that this is one of the most fundamental principles of lean thinking. Better processes, in turn, allow you to offer better service and a better product to your customer. The transformation that 365 is now undergoing—which started with the elimination of inventory and the introduction of flow—has eventually led us to moving our main value creation activities to the shops, which allows us to produce and sell a fresher, healthier product.

While the processes we run in the factory are completely different from those we run in the shops, the basic thinking and values behind both are the same: eliminate waste to provide more value to the customer. Whether we are changing the layout of our production area for better use of the available space or interacting directly with a regular customer from behind a shop's counter, our goal is the same.

"*Todo es una consequencia*," I always say.

Everything is a consequence. A consequence of improving 365 and getting rid of nonvalue-adding activities and waste is, without a doubt, a closer relationship with our customers. Not only are we able to respond more quickly to them and satisfy their needs, but we're also able to develop a closer bond with them and better understand their idea of value. This way we will able to provide more of value to them.

For instance, in the new shop we're now flexible enough to meet more customer needs because we can produce special breads, such as salt-free breads or products for people who are gluten-intolerant. We can also personalize the service we offer. If someone wants a kilogram of dough to make an *empanada gallega* we can provide that.

Our ultimate goal is to make what the customer wants and nothing else. We have great expectations for this new type of shop, which we envision will be a fusion of bread boutique and neighborhood shop.

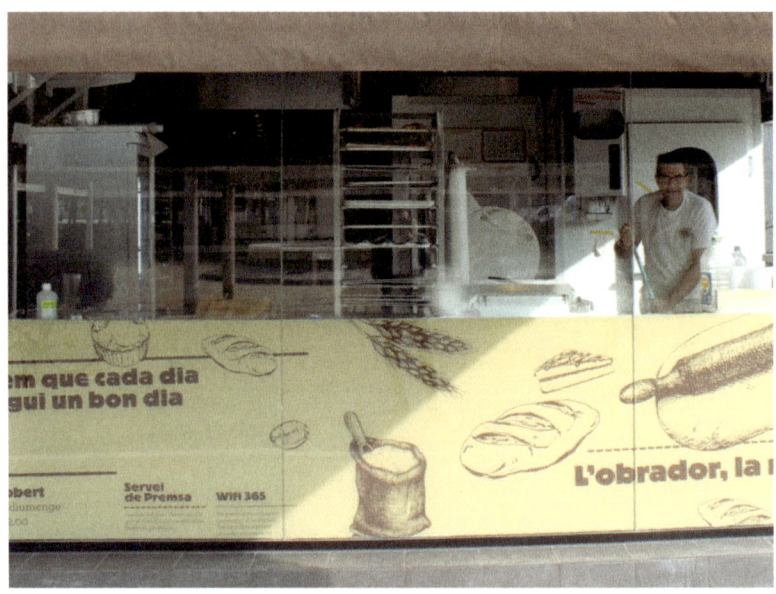

The "mini-factory" of our new shop experiment.

The Process

How can we make this process profitable, and competitive versus economies of scale? By using lean in the same way that Toyota needed in the past to be competitive versus the much bigger automotive competitors.

In its first few months, the new model shop performed poorly and was a total drain. It's located in a working-class neighborhood with no tourists, which provided an extra challenge. But we knew that the lessons we would learn would make the experiment worthwhile. We stayed the course, and I am glad we did. After a fair bit of PDCA, the shop became profitable and we opened a second one, which performed well from the outset.

When 365 began, we had very little space and this forced us to simplify things as much as possible. We continue to use this simplifying approach to keep improvements coming, which in turn fuels the growth of 365. We knew that if we didn't get better, the new shop would not be profitable.

We apply this same drive to improve in our factory. If we want to open 10 new shops in the next year, we know that we need to improve our operations until we are able to comfortably supply an extra 10 shops. Our growth is the incentive we use to improve, and the improvement boosts our growth. The two are mutually reinforcing.

The prevailing approach in our industry is to have mass-produced bread delivered frozen from mega-factories that produce very high volumes—as much as 5,000 loaves an hour.

This results in high costs for transportation, packaging, and storage. In our new shop, we had the opposite problem. We eliminated all the unnecessary costs—we transport only flour, we don't package, and we don't need freezers for storage. But we could produce only what one baker could make.

That's what we worked really hard to improve. Making the new model shop profitable required a lot of adjustments to increase the productivity of the baker and to find the right layout in the back of the shop for the mini-factory. It was a drastic change in process; all the other shops receive either prebaked or frozen bread. This has really taught us to make the most of every situation, to seize every opportunity to learn.

The logistics and layout of the shop made profitability a challenge, but the proximity to the customer and the newly acquired ability to respond to their demands and requirements quickly are simply priceless. For example, natural fermentation (read: higher-quality bread) is something we cannot do in the central factory, because it's busy all night, and we don't have enough space. But in the shop it is possible.

When we first opened the new shop, we had two bakers: one for the morning shift and one for the afternoon shift. Thanks to a number of lean improvements, we managed to increase our productivity. Before long we had a baker working 9–10 hours a day. We further developed the baker's skills and improved the process to make the system better, the shop more profitable, and the working day eight hours long.

We organized and defined all the tasks the baker performs, the exact quantities of all the ingredients needed, and the correct timing for making each product. We tried to turn the space into an environment resembling a production cell. Our objective was to establish flow and a clear sequence for each task, to ensure the product moves easily through the value stream with no interruptions. We added machines, replaced tables (some custom-made to match the height of the machines), placed all

Breaking down the baker's tasks

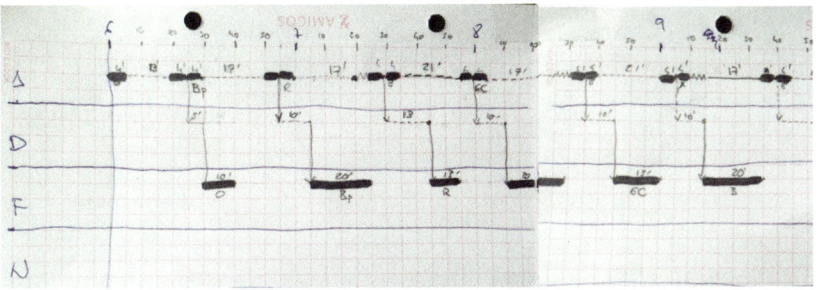

Hand-drawn notes during observation.

Hour	6		7		8		9		10		11		12		...
Mix	O	B	R	B	6C	B	E	X	B	I	P				
Divide		O	B	R	B	6C	B	E	X	B	I	P			
Form			O	B	R	B	6C	B	E	X	B	I	P		
Proofer	24h														
Oven		R	big small		big small		R	big small		big small		R	big small		

Recreated for presentation.

the materials needed in boxes next to the equipment, and started to use carts to transport the different mixes and carry the products to the oven.

It's all about simplifying things. After all, we only need flour and water to make bread. In the new shop, we bring in the flour and then help the baker to combine it with water and his own labor in the most efficient way possible.

The baker had never applied lean thinking before, but after a while he began to follow the standards and measure the time it took him to make the bread, moving himself to our PDCA thinking. We told him that we needed his help to bring the process down to eight hours and that we were there to support him with whatever he might need. Once he got it, he started to push really hard to achieve the goal, creating a continuous set of small kaizens.

The new system gave him a much better work-life balance and completely changed the nature of his work. This probably made the experiment particularly appealing to him. A baker normally works at night producing bread for the same day, but in our new shop he works from 6am–2pm, baking the dough that he made the day before that has just finished fermenting, and preparing the bread for the next day.

In the new shop, our experiments so far have concentrated on bread only, though our plan is to eventually make most of our products there. The bread process is the most complex, so once that is sorted, we expect to be able to find the best approach to produce pastries and cakes pretty quickly.

For the croissants, we plan to transport the triangles of dough to the shop for the baker to shape. The production of cakes will take place entirely in the shop. We already have the machine to whip cream and enough space to accommodate cake production. Because it's only one shop, our production target will be five cakes a day (versus the 500–1,000 we produce each day in the factory), for which we don't need a freezer, just the fridge we already have on site.

One of the difficulties with this system is that we have to combine the process the baker follows with how the place looks in the eye of the customer. The balance is difficult to strike, and sadly, the two things often clash. We couldn't consider only the process and forget the customer; had we done that, the whole experiment would have been pointless. To work out a compromise, we often found ourselves having to move machines around or turning them sideways, even though it meant sacrificing some efficiencies we could have gained.

After all, we are trying to put on a sort of performance for our customers, so that from outside the shop they can see what our baker is doing in real time. Since it seems that everybody is selling bread these days, we think this is way to gain a competitive edge and to give the art of bread making the dignity it deserves.

An Adaptable Success

You can change the process as much and as many times as you want, but you can never afford to lose sight of what goes on in the market. What's really happening out there is the only thing that matters, and lean gives us the flexibility to adapt. Without lean thinking, the new shops would have been completely impossible to manage, and this whole experiment would've failed. We've made many changes, but there is always potential for more improvement, which translates into higher productivity with the same costs.

The new shop model has been a success and we are thinking of converting the other 365 shops to this system in the future. For years, we have been too dependent on the factory, but with the new business model it will lose its *raison d'être*. It will become redundant—not much more than a distribution center that we use to supply the shops, which in turn will become autonomous. All they would need from the factory, acting as a sort of cross-docking system, are third-party products, like soft drinks and mixes.

This is also very much in line with our aspirations to grow outside of Catalonia. With this new, more flexible shop, we can bring 365 to other parts of Spain—and possibly abroad—without having to open new factories, which would be costly and hard to manage. Producing and freezing the bread at the factory and using a refrigerated truck to ship might also work, but the prospect of making a product of a higher quality, producing just what the customer wants, with no logistics and lower costs, is just too appealing.

Quite simply, it's the leanest thing we can do. I see the new shop as the culmination of a learning process—which is not to say we are done learning—and the result of our becoming more mature as a lean organization. Not only are we living up to the idea that removing waste and improving processes brings us closer to our customers, but we are also letting our people gradually take ownership of their work.

Until fairly recently, we made a lot of our products in the factory. However, now that we know that a big part of being a good leader is knowing when to let go of your need to micromanage and control everything, we are making more and more products in the shops—like we have always done with the sandwiches. We trust our people.

More recently, we have recognized the importance of putting the shops at the heart of 365's value creation activity. This necessarily means that we have had to learn to trust the people working in the shops with the many more tasks that they are now asked to perform. Not only do they sell but now they also prepare food and bake the bread. Our new lean shops represent the future of 365, and we want the people working in the shops to be an active part of that.

5. A Different Managerial Culture

When you set out to make improvements and you start to measure the time it takes bakers to complete an action, the first thought in their minds is often that we think they are like slaves, that we are mistreating them, and that they won't even have time to go to the restroom.

New work standards are met with suspicion at first, but after a short while, the scale starts to level. People may still be skeptical, but somehow things start moving. Before long, they realize that, thanks to lean thinking, they are once again owners of their own time, and they will follow the new standard more enthusiastically. This wouldn't be possible if they didn't know that people higher up in the organization, from the production manager all the way up to us, are listening to them and have their best interests at heart.

That's when the lean magic starts to happen. All of a sudden, when a machine breaks, they will notify you about it. When they encounter a problem, they will feel confident and safe enough to flag it—they know they don't need to find excuses.

In a lean organization, you never have the feeling of having to sit up straight when the boss walks in. You don't feel that sense of unease, because you know that you are doing things well, and that any mistake that might occur will just be an opportunity to do better next time.

Raising problems is not only welcomed but encouraged. People are not afraid to tell us that something is not working the way it should, because they know we are there for them and ready to help. In the factory, we have a stand-up meeting every morning at 9:30 to discuss production, the mistakes we made the day before, and other problems. There's no excuse for not speaking up if a machine is acting up or if there is a concern about the production schedule.

In the shops, the meeting is at 6:00am. The manager will say things like, "This has to work this way today, considering the problem we had yesterday. Do you remember we talked about it? This is how we are going to correct it …"

The management system we have facilitates the elevation of problems whenever a solution cannot be found during the morning stand-up meeting. If a shop manager is unable to find a solution with the employees, they call us and either the supervisor goes to the shop or we do.

9:30am factory stand-up meeting

We encourage managers to try to solve problem situations by themselves and we congratulate them when they succeed. But that doesn't mean we don't help them if they are struggling. We do it all the time, while also ensuring we are not spoon-feeding them the answers. If we did that, they would never learn. A manager's role should simply be to oversee an area and help people do their work in the best way possible.

One of the newest ways we have to identify and discuss problems is to write each customer complaint we receive on a piece of paper and then hang all the sheets on the wall at the entrance to the factory, where we normally load products onto delivery trucks. Errors can be anything from a can of soda missing to a loaf of bread slightly burned.

Considering that we deliver 270,000 products every day, one might think the 110–120 mistakes in supply we receive are not a big deal. After all, we are almost talking parts per million! But we take every single error or problem very seriously, to the point that if one baguette is burned, we write down "15,000 burned baguettes" (15,000 is our daily output of baguettes), so that everybody is aware of the magnitude of the problem. As unattainable as perfection might be, we should always be striving for it!

In the problem-solving phase, we analyze what might have led to the issue (*see right*) and where in the process things might have gone wrong. Problems often occur in the warehouse, which is normal: the more you move and handle products, the more likely it will be that some of them might get damaged.

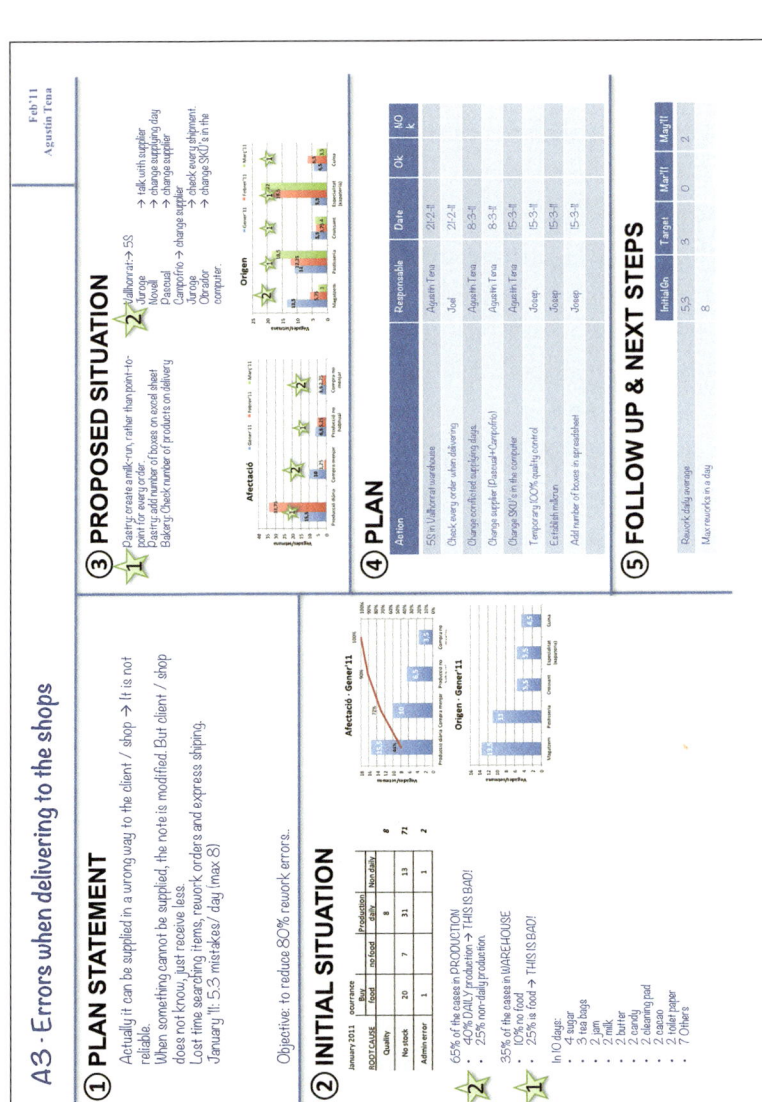

When this happens, people's first reaction is usually to blame the warehouse staff, so we immediately remind them that the department actually needs our help—especially considering that many of its problems are actually caused by errors made upstream—and that finger-pointing is not what we do at 365. We also encourage them to offer ideas and solutions and not simply report problems to be solved.

Easy On the Lean

Lean thinking is absolutely great. It is the reason why 365 has managed to grow so much and so quickly. Yet at times real-life situations must take center stage. At one point, before the employees in the shops really embraced lean thinking, Emi gave me a bit of an ultimatum. "Either my workers start smiling again or this lean thing is out the window!"

This was a good wake-up call for me. It reminded me that you can never lose sight of the real needs of your people and that sometimes you need to give them the time to acclimatize to the new (lean) situation. To me, lean principles made perfect sense from the beginning, but that isn't true for everybody else.

Lean thinking can at times be applied in a very prescriptive manner. But beware, if you "drink too much of the juice," you can easily become a bit intoxicated. You may feel so passionate about lean process improvement that you start pushing ideas down people' throats, but that is counterproductive.

In a lean journey, everybody—from the CEO to the front line—must progress at the right pace. After all, it's a learning process. If change happens in this organic way, there is no limit to what you can achieve when collaborating with your people.

And it's not just with employees that one must be careful: you can have seemingly perfect, very efficient processes, but if your customers are not happy, none of the lean improvements you are making really matter. We had a taste of this in our new shop, the one with the baker making bread "live" in front of passersby. When the machines were turned one way, they worked for the baker—they ensured flow and were part of an optimized process—but when they were turned the other way, they gave customers a better view of the mix being prepared. What to do? It's all a matter of balance. And it begins with value for the customer, not a theoretically optimized process.

Our Culture—The Culmination of What We Do

With the strong foundation (culture) and the bricks (tools) that lean provides us, we can build a house with as many floors as we want. Lean thinking methodology has fueled 365's growth over the past decade or so and given us the ability to adapt to whatever market conditions and challenges we face.

I don't know whether everything we do is "pure lean," but we normally do it anyway. It's just an experiment, after all, and there is nothing wrong with trying something new or different, as long as you have done your math. This means that whatever tool or principle we use must serve our real needs. We don't use all the lean tools all the time, but we have established a basic culture that guides our every move. Sometimes mastering a handful of tools is enough, because ultimately what really matters is your understanding of the principles.

In many ways, as far as lean companies go, we probably look pretty unconventional. If you were to walk into our factory today, your first impression might not be that of having entered a lean firm. The space is confined and there is a lot going on everywhere. We often have to warn people who come to see us before they walk in, "Don't be too fast to judge the place. Let us show you how it works."

The place might not look as visual and orderly as a Toyota plant, but it is cleaned every hour, standards are in place for everything, all our workers know what they are doing, and every task has its time and place.

The very efficient and effective system we have established, with most rooms and machines used for different purposes at different hours of the day, is testament to the culture of improvement we live and breathe. Our complete focus is on constantly delivering value to our customers, whether it means developing a new type of bread or redecorating all of our shops (which we did in 2013).

If I were to identify the five most important ideas driving our transformation, I believe these would be as follows:

1. *Customer focus*—if it doesn't make sense from a customer perspective, we probably shouldn't do it.
2. *Data-driven decision making*—numbers can't be debated.
3. *Problem solving and communication*—there's no excuse for not flagging and discussing an issue.
4. *People engagement*—our job as leaders is to help employees do their jobs better.
5. *Experimentation*—everything can be improved, and mistakes are opportunities to find a better way.

Customer Focus

Listening to the voice of the customer can take many forms. At 365, it means developing a relationship with them and getting to know them (even by name a lot of the time). It also means inviting them to suggest new products and try samples, installing suggestion boxes in our shops, and most important, ensuring that value—and nothing but value—is always created for them. The closer we are to our customers, the more we learn about what we need to do next.

Emi puts it this way: We need to appeal to all of our customers' senses. Our shops need to be presentable (sight), the scent of bread must permeate the street outside (smell), and they need to hear the baker sing or the sound of the mixing machine (hearing), and enjoy the taste of the bread (palate). People won't know how good our bread tastes until they have actually spent their money, so we need to make sure to give them exactly what they want (value) before the purchase. We need to keep this in mind especially at a time when bread is sold everywhere, from supermarkets to gas stations.

Data-driven Decision Making

We have a lot of faith in numbers. We need them to assess the company's performance but also to set and adjust our targets.

Data and facts drive our decision-making process. For example, imagine that improvements reveal that a shop would function better with two workers instead of three. The moment we tell the employees that one of them will be going to a different shop, they will start coming up with reasons why that can't work. But when we explain this change using numbers and targets, they quickly understand why a third person is not needed and how the shop can function well with two people.

You tell them, "Your target is to sell this much, and you are already doing this by yourself in the morning. Your colleague is doing the same in the afternoon." The facts are indisputable. And of course people are reallocated.

Problem Solving and Communication

Solving a problem, like making an improvement or launching a new product, requires a good system of communication.

In the management structure we've created, information travels fast through the layers of the business, and frequent and direct interaction occurs between people in the factory and at the shops. Communication is a natural part of the way we work.

Because we strive to learn from our mistakes, we are trying to improve the role and capabilities of middle management. When Unai or one of the shop supervisors sits down with the teams to discuss problems, we're trying to surface employees' opinions. This fosters a culture of teamwork and creates trust, which in turn encourages our people to own the improvement ideas they come up with and see them through.

People Engagement

You can't successfully engage your people until you manage to make them feel like they are working in a safe environment. They need to know they can raise an issue or make an improvement without being harassed, shushed, or ridiculed. The safer they feel, the more they will support you and your improvement attempts.

Needless to say, the result of an improvement can never be a layoff. If you sack someone upon the realization that you need only two of the three people you have, what you will get the next time you try to implement lean is a resounding NO!

The efficiencies we identify never result in layoffs; instead, we use those extra resources elsewhere, in another place where value needs to be added. We also tend to give those people a higher purpose, for example, helping a shop that is struggling or coming up with new ways to bring value to customers.

Experimentation

I always say you can regret only one thing and that is not having tried. I have found that most of the time it is cheaper to test an idea and make a mistake than it is to spend three months thinking about it. We are constantly running experiments at 365. We strongly believe that trying new things is the best, if not the only, way to learn.

For example, we recently opened a shop in the town of Figueres, located 150 kilometers from Barcelona. This is costing a lot of money, but we are learning a lot. If the shop is a success and the system we put in place to supply it works, we'll know that we can open up more shops within a 150-km radius. This experiment is helping us to explore another way to grow, as PDCA cycles get us closer and closer to where we want to go.

Our cultural framework has made us strong enough to not only survive, but even grow during the worst years of the 2008 global financial crisis. This was the second crisis I experienced as an entrepreneur, and the two could not have been more different. I now realize that the 1992 crisis, which resulted in the demise of the bakeries my family ran, was mostly our own. We were putting our hearts and souls into the development of the business, but we didn't have control over our processes and costs, and so the business eventually folded.

Conversely, in 2008 we not only survived but opened six new shops. We faced this economic crisis fully aware of the weapons at our disposal. This time, we were in control of our processes and knew what we were doing. If the markets are in turmoil and sales drop, you need to make decisions quickly, and lean gives you all the tools you need to be responsive.

Lean thinking gives us the flexibility we need to adapt to changing situations and fuel our growth. It gives us control of our processes through the standards we implement and continuously improve. If our shop assistants know that they are in control, they'll be able to approach any situation calmly and effectively, which makes our customers happy. And we all know that happier customers are faithful customers.

6. How 365 Experiments

Here is an example of how we experiment and problem solve at 365, captured in two matrices, shown here and on page 92–93.

1. Background

Capacity issue and high losses due to products going bad after sitting in the freezer for too long.

2. Initial Condition

Production happens in weekly batches following economies-of-scale mentality. Our freezer is always too full, and our forecasts never match the reality of how much we need to produce. Product traceability is a challenge.

3. Proposed Condition

Produce every day just what is needed.

4. Plan

Level and standardize the schedule.
Reduce batch size to minimum.

5. Follow-up

PDCA batch quantities to reduce to right size.
Confirm that freezer not needed.

Initial condition	Your idea	What you tried
Round 1	Limit production to what is needed the following day.	Ask bakers to produce only what is needed for the next day.
Round 2	Limit production to what is needed the following day.	Take away all the trolleys except those needed to meet daily demand.
Round 3	Improve the flow in the bakery.	Paint lines on floor. Encourage people to follow flow and pull trolleys when they're ready for the next step in the process.
Round 4	Eliminate non-value added activities to reduce lead-time in production.	Remove the freezer from the production area (no longer needed because batches are smaller).

What happened	What next?
People were afraid and continued to work the usual way.	Understand why people are resisting and think of another experiment.
Completed daily production, but push mentality (not single-trolley flow) created waiting in other tasks.	No inventory anymore, but this system doesn't create flow. Need to create a new experiment.
This worked and people started to pull.	Some parts of the process are not needed any longer, so future improvements will focus on simplifying it.
Eliminating the bottleneck reduced lead-time and freed up capacity in the bakery.	Continuous improvement of the value stream map.

Your Turn

Now it's time to try your own experiment. Draw the templates below and at right and experiment with *Zero Stockout Inventory Reduction*. Or decide on a problem you'd like to experiment with and get to work. *Bon profit!*

1. Background	3. Proposed Condition
2. Initial Condition	4. Plan
	5. Follow-up

Zero Stockout Inventory Reduction

Break down one week of your inventory into seven parts (or six if you're closed one day), and experiment to reduce inventory, increase flexibility, and improve freshness through learning your true demand/usage rates.

Initial condition	Your idea	What you tried	What happened	What next?
Round 1				
Round 2				
Round 3				

Conclusion

A lean journey is never-ending. It takes you places you never thought you'd go and constantly surprises you with all the things it helps you discover. Our lean journey at 365 may never end, but it certainly had a clear start. The decision to go down the lean route was a result of my own unrest—following the mistakes I had made and all that I experienced over the years—and the lack of structure that characterized the way we ran our business.

As I mentioned at the start of this book, it is important to face a difficult situation with the right tools in hand. Sadly, the default response of many senior managers to disappointing financial results or problems their companies encounter is still to blame people, ask them to work harder, and then retreat to the safety of their offices. Instead, they should focus on how broken their processes are and on fixing them with their people at the gemba.

If people are to thrive, they must be allowed to operate in a system that encourages them to expose and solve problems, improve their work, and collaborate with their colleagues on creating value. This is easier said than done. for many years, I made the mistake of thinking that hard work alone would result in the success of my business. How naive of me!

For those of us who have been lucky enough to discover lean thinking, there is hope. The philosophy and methodology give us profoundly effective ways to turn waste into value for our customers by leveraging the knowledge of our employees and improving our processes. Too often, however, we fall into the trap of thinking that lean is just some kind of recipe, that if followed correctly will magically turn our companies into the next Toyota. It isn't.

Lean thinking provides an alternative approach to managing your business, and its principles must be understood and adapted to your own circumstances. It is hard work; many try and very few succeed. This is not to say that we have "made it" or that we are the "Toyota of baguettes." Far from it. We make so many mistakes all the time. Like I said, it took someone from outside of 365 to show us how much we have accomplished, which eventually led to writing this book.

What we have managed to build at 365, is the idea that failure should be encouraged, because from it comes improvement. If we are to ensure that failure doesn't destroy our businesses we must learn to "contain" it. To quote Jim Womack (on *PlanetLean.org*), this means running "experiments that are bounded and that can give rapid answers as to whether the proposed ideas will actually work and benefit the organization."

Experimentation is, I believe, the most important practice that lean has taught us, and probably the most important takeaway from this book. When we introduce a new product, move a machine in our factory, change our production system, or even open a new type of shop (some experiments are bigger than others), all we are trying to do is test our assumptions and gradually build the knowledge we need to grow our business.

Lean thinking inspires us to strive for systemic change—even though we know we might never get there—through incremental change. The world around us changes all the time, and our businesses must learn to keep up if they are to stay competitive. Without trying new things, there can be no innovation. So, experiment as much as you can, don't be afraid to fail, and make sure there is always learning to be gained.

I hope this book has showed you how useful and powerful lean experiments can be and has perhaps encouraged you to try a few of your own. Whether you design software, produce cars, or care for patients, experiments represent the lifeblood of your lean transformation. Without them, there can be no improvement—just like there can be no bread without flour.

About the Authors

Juan Antonio Tena

Juan Antonio Tena is the CEO of 365, a chain of 100 cafés and bakeries in Barcelona.

His professional experience spans different industries. Over the years, he has worked as a milling machine operator for car-maker SEAT in Barcelona, and even run a trucking company with his brothers. His passion, however, has always been in cafés and bread-making. In 2000, he started 365 with his wife Emi. After reading *Lean Thinking* in 2004, he started a journey that completely transformed the organization and his approach to managing it.

Juan Antonio holds a master's degree in management from IESE Business School.

Emi Castro

Emi Castro is the Retail Manager at 365, a chain of 100 cafés and bakeries in Barcelona.

Emi had her first job at 15—every weekend she worked in a fruit shop, where she first discovered her passion for selling and interacting with customers. At 25, she took a diploma in social studies to improve her ability to understand and interact with people. In 2000, she started 365 with her husband Juan Antonio. Today, Emi is responsible for running the network of 365 shops. She has been instrumental in bringing lean thinking to the retail side of the business.

Lean Enterprise Institute

LEI is a nonprofit education, publishing, and management research organization, founded in 1997 by lean management expert, Jim Womack, Ph.D. LEI's mission is to promote the principles of lean thinking and practice across a wide range of manufacturing and service industries to help organizations transform themselves into lean enterprises. LEI books, online products, and workshops teach lean methods and principles, and assist lean leaders in developing the behaviors necessary to create and sustain lean enterprises. LEI Summits highlight organizations in the process of making lean breakthroughs. LEI is also a member of the Lean Global Network.

Visit us at: **lean.org**

Instituto Lean Management

Based in Barcelona, Catalonia, Spain, we are a non-profit association established by a group of professionals and experts in lean thinking. Our mission is to extend LEAN MANAGEMENT and its implementation, in all sectors of the economy and all functions of companies, through conferences, publications, and education workshops—as well as the development of research-based, lean, co-learning projects. ILM is also a member of the Lean Global Network.

Visit us at: **institutolean.org**